P9-DTB-738

29.95

Paper Cutouts

by

Hélène Leroux-Hugon
and Juliette Vicart

A FIREFLY BOOK

Published by Firefly Books Ltd. 2007

Copyright © 2007 Edilarge S.A., Editions Ouest France, Rennes

All rights reserved. No part of this publication may be reproduced, stored in a retrieval system, or transmitted in any form or by any means, electronic, mechanical, photocopying, recording or otherwise, without the prior written permission of the Publisher.

First printing

Publisher Cataloging-in-Publication Data (U.S.)

Leroux-Hugon, Hélène.
    Paper cutouts / Hélène Leroux-Hugon and Juliette Vicart ; photographs by Xavier Scheinkmann.
[106] p. : col. ill. , col. photos. ; cm.
Includes bibliographical references.
Summary: Paper cut designs for the modern home which reflect the artistry of traditional Chinese ornamentation. These motifs can be used as framed elegant works of art or applied to walls or furniture.
ISBN-13: 978-1-55407-320-7
ISBN-10: 1-55407-320-0
1. Paper work. 2. Paper work–China. I. Vicart, Juliette. II.Scheinkmann, Xavier. III. Title.
745.54 dc22   TT870.L476 2007

Library and Archives Canada Cataloguing in Publication

Leroux-Hugon, Hélène
    Paper cutouts / Hélène Leroux-Hugon and Juliette
Vicart ; photographs by Xavier Scheinkmann.
Includes bibliographical references.
ISBN-13: 978-1-55407-320-7
ISBN-10: 1-55407-320-0
    1. Paper work. 2. Decoupage. I. Vicart, Juliette. II. Title.

TT870.L47 2007   736'.98   C2007-902141-7

Published in the United States by
Firefly Books (U.S.) Inc.
P.O. Box 1338, Ellicott Station
Buffalo, New York 14205

Published in Canada by
Firefly Books Ltd.
66 Leek Crescent
Richmond Hill, Ontario L4B 1H1

Editor: Catherine Dandres Franck
Assistant Editor: Hélène Pouchot
Photoengraving: Micro Lynx, Rennes (35)

Design, layout and cover: Bleu T, Paris

Printed in France - L43531

Acknowledgments

The authors and the publisher would like to thank Magali Le Mansec and Claudine Bracigliano of La cachette d'Ali Babette *for their warm welcome while photos were taken in their lovely little shop.*

Hélène Leroux-Hugon

and

Juliette Vicart

Paper Cutouts

PHOTOGRAPHS BY XAVIER SCHEINKMANN

FIREFLY BOOKS

Table of Contents

The Patterns

736.98
LER
2007

Introduction

Historical Overview of Paper Cutouts

Based on archeological excavations carried out in China, the origins of paper cutting may date back as far as 2,000 years before Christ.

Practiced by Chinese peasants during festivals and major life events, the art of paper cutting was first inspired by symbols of good luck, then, gradually, by flowers, landscapes and scenes of everyday life. Passed on by generation after generation of women, this art form continues to thrive throughout Asia, especially during the celebration of spring marking the Chinese New Year. In Japan, the same technique can be found in *kirie* (paper cutouts), *kirigami* (pieces of paper folded and cut out) and *katagami* (stencils for fabrics).

Although traditionally associated with Asia, this technique is a form of popular expression that has flourished throughout Europe and the Americas in a variety of ways, but always in connection with celebrations.

For example, according to Jewish tradition, the *ketubah*, or marriage contract, is made of paper that has been cut out, written on in calligraphy and painted. Paper lace pictures are offered at bar mitzvahs.

In South America, the streets and houses are adorned with motifs drawn on colored paper and shaped by a cutout or a punched hole. Polish farmers decorate their houses with colorful *wycinanki*, comprised of simple or more complicated motifs and inspired by everyday events. The German *scherenschnitte* and the Dutch *papiersnyden* show sharply defined peasant scenes cut out of black or white paper.

At the end of the 17th century, nuns in France, Germany and Switzerland cut out pious lacy images called *canivets* using a penknife. In 18th century France, the silhouette portrait grew out of the caricatures of the very unpopular minister of finance at the time, Étienne de Silhouette. Two Swiss artists, Johann Jacob Hauswirth (1809–1871), a woodcutter, and Louis Saugy (1871–1953), a mailman and farmer, folded and cut out magnificent scenes of rural life and climbs to mountain pastures.

These few details on the history of paper cutting are offered to the reader who, upon discovering this art form, would like to learn more about it.

Choice of Paper

Used as a support for graphic design and color, paper is a material that offers a great deal of variety in texture, pattern and grain. It invites us to fold it and cut it. More than ever before, paper is used by artists and graphic designers alike, whether amateur or professional.

Paper has many characteristics and there's a wide variety to choose from: paper with a grain, paper without a grain, Japanese paper, Nepalese paper… The list goes on and on. The type of paper you choose is essential and depends on the artistic technique you wish to use.

For paper cutouts such as the ones proposed in this book, choose low-weight paper without a grain, as this will make it easier to fold and cut. Also, it's better to use colorfast paper; it will be a shame if the color of your cutout fades in the light. The size of the sheet of paper will be determined by the pattern you want to make.

How to Proceed

Tools

→ cutting mat

→ direct light on the working area, since cutting out paper tires the eyes

→ small embroidery scissors or small precision scissors, curved or straight (sold in craft stores)

→ art knife, craft knife or scalpel

→ hole punches in different sizes to shape eyes, berries or flowers

→ adhesive tape or paperclips to hold the paper in place

→ repositionable spray adhesive

→ bookbinding adhesive

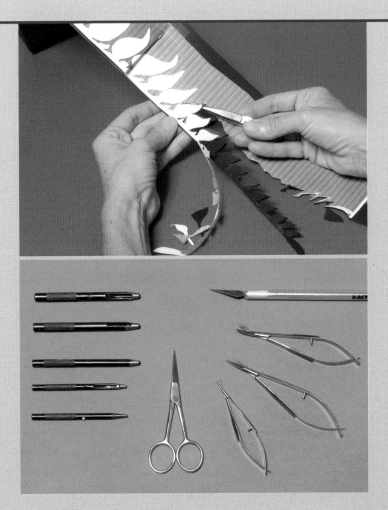

Choice of Pattern

The technique of paper cutouts, just like stenciling, requires carefully thinking out the shape, composition, framing and balance between solids and spaces. The outlines and large surface areas that remain uncut create a visual balance. They also reinforce the small surface areas and extremely delicate cutouts. It's a good idea to alternate them. The pattern you choose must be stylized, clear and arranged with care.

The primary difficulty in making paper cutouts lies in creating links that are regular throughout the motif and wide enough to ensure the individual parts of the pattern are sufficiently strong to hold together the entire cutout once it's finished. In the design shown on pages 8 and 9, these small links are actually the feet of the insects, which join them to the flowers and the leaves.

These connectors, or bridges, add strength to the cutout and beauty to the motif. In the Tree of Dancing Rabbits (pages 20–21) the rabbits' ears hold the arabesques of the tree together. These elements play both a structural and an aesthetic role. If the pattern selected appears to be too delicate and, therefore, too fragile, simply enlarge it using a photocopier in order to reinforce the small elements.

The motifs proposed in this book are framed inside square, round or oval borders, like the Japanese *kakemono*. You can choose the appropriate shape depending on your project. Gather information and various samples, do research in books and museum catalogues, and look for inspiration in the traditional paper cutouts from places such as China, Austria and Persia.

How to Proceed

Drawing and Folding

Once you have selected a pattern, you can either draw it directly onto the paper to be cut—folded or not depending on the pattern—or trace it and transfer it later.

However, before you trace the design, ask yourself how you're going to proceed: will this be a simple, straightforward cutout made from unfolded paper? Or will the pattern be cut out of folded paper and appear in full, perhaps repeated several times over, once the paper is unfolded?

Another technique for transferring a pattern involves tracing it on fine typewriter or photocopy paper, then holding it in place on top of the paper to be cut using adhesive tape or paperclips. You simply move the paperclips as you cut.

Some of the cutouts shown in this book are made with paper that is folded in two, three or four, while others use unfolded paper. Some paper cutouts combine folded and unfolded paper. Cat-in-an-Egg uses both. To start, you cut out the border of the paper while it is folded in two, then you unfold it and cut the central motif out of a single thickness of paper.

1 Pattern on paper folded in four.

2 Pattern on paper folded in two.

The finished
pattern.

How to Proceed

Designing a Single Symmetrical Pattern

In the case of a single pattern such as Tree of Life, Persian Cypresses and Beetles, the motif is cut out of a sheet of paper folded in two. The pattern is drawn on only one side of the folded paper, with the center of the motif lined up along the fold so that the whole pattern appears once it's cut out and the paper unfolded.

Designing a Frieze

To create a frieze from a single pattern, you can trace the design on several sheets of unfolded paper and glue the cutouts together by placing them side by side, or you can reproduce the design on folded paper—just ensure the ends of the traced design, at the edges of the paper, are wide enough to create a bridge. Once the pattern is cut out, unfold the paper and you'll have as many patterns as there are thicknesses of paper. Depending on the weight of the paper, it can be folded in two, three, four, five or even six.

In the case of By the Side of the Road, Farm and Underwater Frieze, when enough copies of the pattern are cut out you can create a frieze to decorate a child's bedroom wall, a bathroom or even the kitchen.

Designing a Round

In most of the round examples the pattern is transferred to one quarter of a circle of paper 16 inches (40 cm) in diameter and folded in four before cutting. The paper for Round of Two Carps, which shows a symmetrical pattern, is folded in two. Nasturtiums, shown opposite and on page 97, is the exception: this pattern was cut without folding the paper because it does not need to be symmetrical.

Cutting

Cutting techniques vary depending on whether you are cutting the outline or the central motif. We recommend that you start by cutting out the central elements using an art or craft knife, scalpel or small precision scissors, and finish by cutting the outline of the motif.

Cutting with a Scalpel

The use of a scalpel, art, or craft knife (do not use a utility knife, it's not accurate enough), essentially involves cutting out small patterns from unfolded paper, but you can also use this technique with folded paper. However, working with several thicknesses of paper is more difficult because it requires more strength. Fortunately, the sharpness of the scalpel blade helps to make a good cut.

Take the paper on which the design has been transferred, place it on the cutting mat and hold it with one hand. With the other hand, cut out the motifs using the scalpel or art knife, holding it like you would a pen. The handiness of this tool allows for accurate hand movements and the careful cutting of tiny pencil markings. Use with care to avoid injury.

Cutting with Scissors

Small embroidery scissors are well adapted to cutting outlines. Small precision scissors, however, help to cut out small, rounded shapes, as well as more complicated outlines, or to remove thinner paper, which is harder for its blades to cut. When you encounter this type of problem, there's a very simple way to get around it: use a hole punch and hit it with a hammer or a small wooden mallet to punch a hole in the surface to be cut out. Insert the blades of the scissors into the hole and continue cutting along the pencil line.

Gluing

➜ Repositionable spray adhesive is helpful, but it needs to be used with care because the vaporized spray is not accurate. This adhesive does, however, allow you to temporarily glue small cutouts onto different types of supports.

➜ To glue a frieze, first mark the desired position on the wall using a pencil. Paste the first 8 inches (20 cm) of the frieze in place then, holding the frieze against the wall, progressively glue on the rest, protecting the wall and the frieze with a sheet of paper. Use a dull varnish to seal it.

➜ Quick-drying gel adhesive is used differently. Make the markings then place small drops of glue at regular intervals on the motif, starting at the top or the bottom. For patterns that include trees, start with the trunk and follow along up the branches.

➜ Quick-drying white vinyl adhesive, the type used for bookbinding, is applied directly onto the frieze using a fine paintbrush. It's colorless and recommended for longer adhesion.

➜ To paste a large central motif, start at the top and gradually add thumbtacks to hold it in place while the adhesive dries.

The
Patterns

Round of Swans

Paper: smooth, white or colored, colorfast, 20 lb. (or 80 gsm)

Dimensions, unfolded: 15 3/4-in. (40 cm) diameter

Tools: small precision scissors and 1/16-, 1/8- and 1/6-in. (2, 3 and 4 mm) hole punches

Folding: in four

Cutting: cut out the motif and finish with the outline.

14

Paper: smooth, white or colored, colorfast, 20 lb. (or 80 gsm)

Dimensions, unfolded: 15 3/4-in. (40 cm) diameter

Tools: small precision scissors and 1/16-, 1/8- and 1/6-in. (2, 3 and 4 mm) hole punches

Folding: in four

Cutting: cut out the motif and finish with the outline.

Round of Angels

Paper: smooth, white or colored, colorfast, 20 lb. (or 80 gsm)

Dimensions, unfolded: 15 3/4-in. (40 cm) diameter

Tools: small precision scissors and 1/16-, 1/8- and 1/6-in. (2, 3 and 4 mm) hole punches

Folding: in four

Cutting: cut out the motif and finish with the outline.

16

Round of Amorous Elves

Paper: smooth, white or colored, colorfast, 20 lb. (or 80 gsm)

Dimensions, unfolded: 15 3/4-in. (40 cm) diameter

Tools: small precision scissors and 1/16-, 1/8- and 1/6-in. (2, 3 and 4 mm) hole punches

Folding: in four

Cutting: cut out the motif and finish with the outline.

Paper: smooth, white or colored, colorfast, 20 lb. (or 80 gsm)

Dimensions, unfolded: 10 x 11¾ in. (25 x 30 cm)

Tools: small precision scissors and ¹⁄₁₆-in. (2 mm) hole punch

Folding: in two

Cutting: cut out the motif and finish with the outline.

Keep the connectors between the trunk, branches and flowers to hold the cutout together.

SIMMS LIBRARY
ALBUQUERQUE ACADEMY

Tree of Dancing Rabbits

Paper: smooth, white, 20 lb.
(or 80 gsm)

Dimensions, unfolded: 10 x 15¾-in. (25 x 40 cm)

Tools: small precision scissors, art knife or scalpel
and ¹⁄₁₆-in. (2 mm) hole punch

Folding: in two

Cutting: cut out the motif and finish with the outline.

Keep the connectors between the trunk, branches
and rabbits to hold the cutout together.

21

Tree of Doves

Paper: smooth, white, 20 lb. (or 80 gsm)

Dimensions, unfolded: 9¹⁄₂ x 11 in. (24 x 28 cm)

Tools: small precision scissors, art knife or scalpel and ¹⁄₁₆-in. (2 mm) hole punch

Folding: in two

Cutting: cut out the motif and finish with the outline.

Noah's Tree

Paper: smooth, white, 20 lb. (or 80 gsm)

Dimensions, unfolded: 10 x 11 in. (25 x 28 cm)

Tools: small precision scissors, art knife or scalpel and $1/16$-in. (2 mm) hole punch

Folding: in two

Cutting: cut out the motif and finish with the outline.

Keep the connectors between the trunk, branches and animals to hold the cutout together.

Underwater Frieze

Paper: smooth, orange, colorfast, 20 lb. (or 80 gsm)

Dimensions, unfolded: 9 1/2 x 28 1/4 in. (24 x 72 cm)

Tools: small precision scissors, art knife or scalpel and 1/32- and 1/16-in. (1 and 2 mm) hole punches

Folding: in two, four or six

Cutting: cut out the motif and finish with the outline.

Keep some of the connectors among the seaweed to hold the cutout together.

To create a longer frieze, cut out several copies or thicknesses of the pattern.

24

By the Side of the Road

Paper: Japanese, smooth, green, colorfast, 20 lb. (80 gsm)

Dimensions, unfolded: 9 1/2 x 37 3/4 in. (24 x 96 cm)

Tools: small precision scissors, art knife or scalpel and 1/32- and 1/16-in. (1 and 2 mm) hole punches

Folding: in two, four or six

Cutting: cut out the motif and finish with the outline.

Keep the connectors between the flowers and blades of grass to hold the cutout together.

To create a longer frieze, cut out several copies or thicknesses of the pattern.

Queen Anne's Lace

Paper: smooth, white, 20 lb. (or 80 gsm)

Dimensions, laid flat: 9 1/2 x 28 1/4 in. (24 x 72 cm)

Tools: small precision scissors, art knife or scalpel and 1/16-in. (2 mm) hole punch

Cutting: cut out the motif and finish with the outline.

Keep the connectors between the stems and leaves to hold the cutout together.

To create a longer frieze, cut out several copies or thicknesses of the pattern.

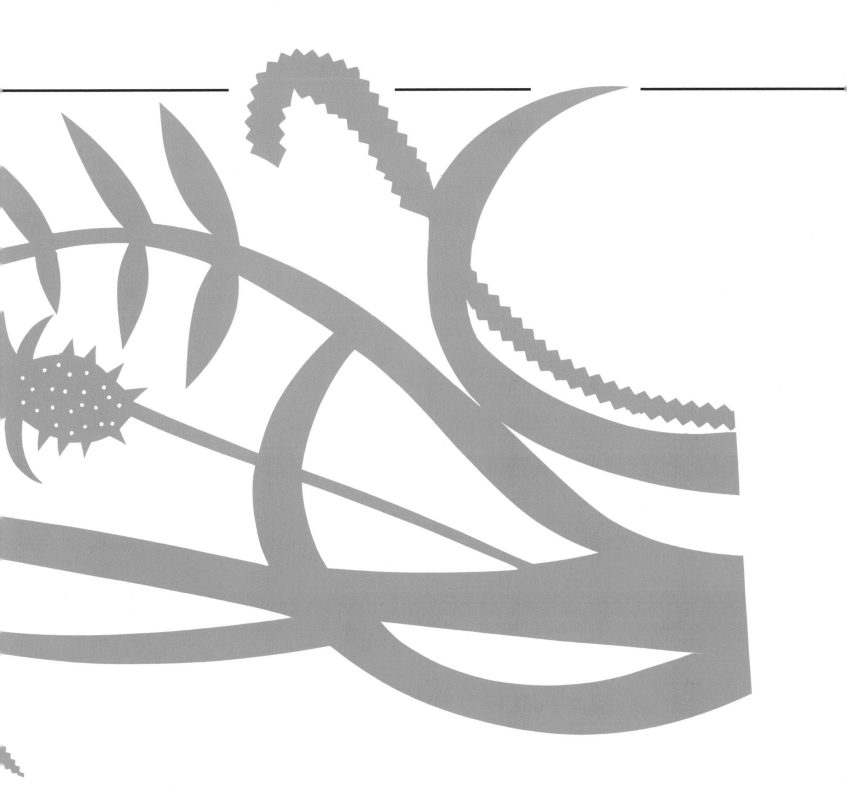

◁ **Underwater Frieze, displayed**

By the Side of the Road, displayed △

Spring

Paper: smooth, pale green, colorfast, 20 lb. (or 80 gsm)

Dimensions, unfolded: 9 1/2 x 15 3/4 in. (24 x 40 cm)

Tools: small precision scissors and art knife or scalpel

Folding: in two

Cutting: cut out the motif and finish with the outline.

If necessary, enlarge the pattern using a photocopier.

Summer

Paper: smooth, orange, colorfast, 20 lb. (or 80 gsm)

Dimensions unfolded: 9 1/2 x 15 3/4 in. (24 x 40 cm)

Tools: small precision scissors and art knife or scalpel

Folding: in two

Cutting: cut out the motif and finish with the outline.

If necessary, enlarge the pattern using a photocopier.

Fall

Paper: smooth, plum, colorfast, 20 lb. (or 80 gsm)

Dimensions unfolded: 9½ x 15¾ in. (24 x 40 cm)

Tools: small precision scissors and art knife or scalpel

Folding: in two

Cutting: cut out the motif and finish with the outline.

If necessary, enlarge the pattern using a photocopier.

Paper: smooth, gray, colorfast, 20 lb. (or 80 gsm)

Dimensions unfolded: 9 1/2 x 15 3/4 in. (24 x 40 cm)

Tools: small precision scissors and art knife or scalpel

Folding: in two

Cutting: cut out the motif and finish with the outline.

If necessary, enlarge the pattern using a photocopier.

Cat-in-an-Egg

Paper: smooth, white or colored, colorfast, 20 lb. (or 80 gsm)

Dimensions, unfolded:
11 x 7 in. (28 x 18 cm)

Tools: small precision scissors

Folding: fold the paper in two to cut out the mice around the border, then unfold the paper to cut out the central motif.

Cutting: cut out the motif and finish with the outline.

To make Cat-in-an-Egg, first fold the paper to make the border, then unfold it to cut out the central motif and the two mice along the fold.

Paper: smooth, white or colored, colorfast, 20 lb. (or 80 gsm)

Dimensions, unfolded: 11x 7 in. (28 x 18 cm)

Tools: small precision scissors

Folding: fold the paper in two to cut out the central motif and the border, then unfold it to cut out the chicks around the border.

Cutting: cut out the motif and finish with the outline.

Monogrammed Hearts

Paper: smooth, white, 20 lb. (or 80 gsm)

Dimensions, unfolded: 6 x 5 1/2 in. (15 x 14 cm)

Tools: small precision scissors and art knife or scalpel

Cutting: cut out the motif and finish with the outline.

Christmas Tree

Paper: smooth, red, colorfast, 20 lb. (or 80 gsm)

Dimensions, unfolded: 18 1/2 x 18 1/2 in. (47 x 47 cm)

Tools: small precision scissors, art knife or scalpel and 1/16- and 1/8-in. (2 and 3 mm) hole punches

Folding: in two

Cutting: follow the design and cut out.

Farm

Paper: smooth, brown, colorfast, 20 lb. (or 80 gsm)

Dimensions, unfolded: 9 ½ x 28 ¼ in. (24 x 72 cm)

Tools: small precision scissors and art knife or scalpel

Folding: in two or, to lengthen the frieze, in four

Cutting: cut out the motif and finish with the outline.

To create a longer frieze, cut out several copies or thicknesses of the pattern.

Climb to Mountain Pastures

Paper: smooth, black, colorfast, 20 lb. (or 80 gsm)

Dimensions, unfolded: 9 1/2 x 37 3/4 in. (24 x 96 cm)

Tools: art knife or scalpel

Cutting: cut out the motif and finish with the outline.

To create the motif of chalets and trees, either cut out of several thicknesses, or cut out several copies and place them side-by-side like a garland.

The Climb to Mountain Pastures can be enlarged by cutting out of paper folded in two or three, provided you choose a low-weight paper, 20 lb. (or 80 gsm) at the most. You will recognize whole chalet and tree patterns forming as you unfold the paper.

Enlarging this motif to 200% with a photocopier will produce a large wall panel, which looks nice in a chalet.

Farmyard

Paper: smooth, red, colorfast, 20 lb. (or 80 gsm)

Dimensions, unfolded: 9 ½ x 18 in. (24 x 46 cm)

Tools: small precision scissors and art knife or scalpel

Folding: in two, four or six

Cutting: cut out the motif and finish with the outline.

◁ **Climb to Mountain Pastures, displayed**

Farmyard, displayed △

Dandelion

Paper: smooth, black, colorfast, 20 lb. (or 80 gsm)

Dimensions, laid flat: 8 x 10 1/4 in. (20 x 26 cm)

Tools: small precision scissors and art knife or scalpel

Folding: in two

Cutting: cut out the motif and finish with the outline.

To make a longer frieze, cut out several copies or thicknesses of the pattern using folded paper and keeping the connectors intact.

Fish among Water Lilies

Paper: smooth, white, 20 lb. (or 80 gsm)

Dimensions, laid flat: 9½ x 9½ in. (24 x 24 cm)

Tools: small precision scissors, art knife or scalpel and ¹⁄₁₆-in. (2 mm) hole punch

Folding: in two

Cutting: cut out the motif and finish with the outline.

Keep the connectors between the leaves and fish to hold the cutout together.

Two Cranes Face-to-Face

Paper: smooth, white, 20 lb. (or 80 gsm)

Dimensions, unfolded: 9 1/2 x 9 1/2 in. (24 x 24 cm)

Tools: small precision scissors, art knife or scalpel and 1/16-in (2 mm) hole punch

Cutting: cut out the pattern and finish with the outline.

Keep the connectors between the ornaments and cranes to hold the cutout together.

Poppy Hanging Lamp

Paper: untearable, white

Dimensions, unfolded cutouts: 19 x 29 ½ in. (48 x 75 cm) for the larger cutout and 19 x 19 ¾ in. (48 x 50 cm) for the two smaller ones

Tools: art knife or scalpel

Folding: in four and six

Cutting: cut out the motif and finish with the outline.

This hanging lamp is made using three cutouts placed one on top of the other. The pattern is cut out of a sheet of paper folded in six for the first cutout, and in four for the other two.

The different paper thicknesses are placed on a support that keeps the paper away from the light bulb, which should have a low wattage.

Bird and Branch

Paper: Japanese, black, patterned

Dimensions, laid flat:
8³/₄ x 20³/₄ in.
(22 x 53 cm)

Tools: art knife or scalpel

Cutting: cut out the motif and finish with the outline.

Glue this pattern to one side of a folding screen (see also p. 68).

Wisteria

Paper: Japanese, orange

Dimensions, laid flat: 11½ x 13¾ in. (30 x 35 cm)

Tools: art knife or scalpel

Cutting: cut out the motif and finish with the outline.

Glue this pattern to the other side of the folding screen (see p. 67).

Two Herons

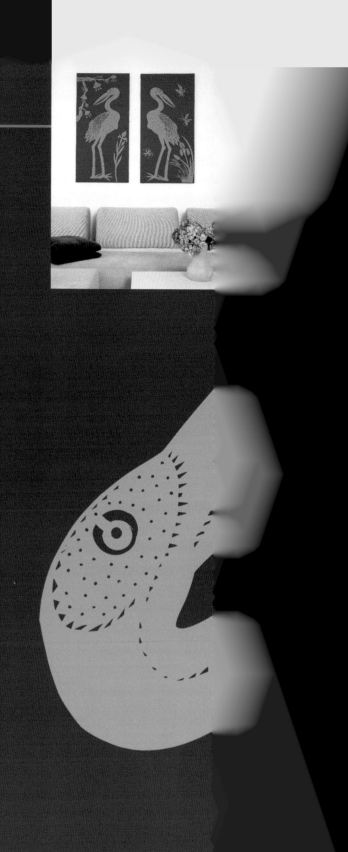

Paper: smooth, orange, colorfast, 20 lb. (or 80 gsm)

Dimensions, one heron laid flat:
32 1/4 x 12 1/2 in. (82 x 32 cm)

Tools: small precision scissors, art knife or scalpel and 1/16- and 1/8-in. (2 and 3 mm) hole punches

Cutting: cut out the motif and finish with the outline.

Cut out several copies of the pattern on either separate sheets of paper or on a stack of sheets.

Two herons on two stretched canvasses are displayed at the upper right. Plum or purple acrylic paint was rolled onto the canvas before the cutout was glued on.

Two Dragons

Paper: Japanese, red, with honeycomb pattern

Dimensions, one dragon: 9 1/2 x 37 3/4 in. (24 x 96 cm)

Tools: small precision scissors, art knife or scalpel and 1/32- and 1/16-in. (1 and 2 mm) hole punches

Cutting: cut out the motif and finish with the outline.

Cut out several copies of the pattern on either separate sheets of paper or on a stack of sheets.

The dragons were cut out of red Japanese paper and displayed on a 20 3/4 x 70 3/4 in. (53 x 180 cm) piece of grained eggplant-colored wallpaper.

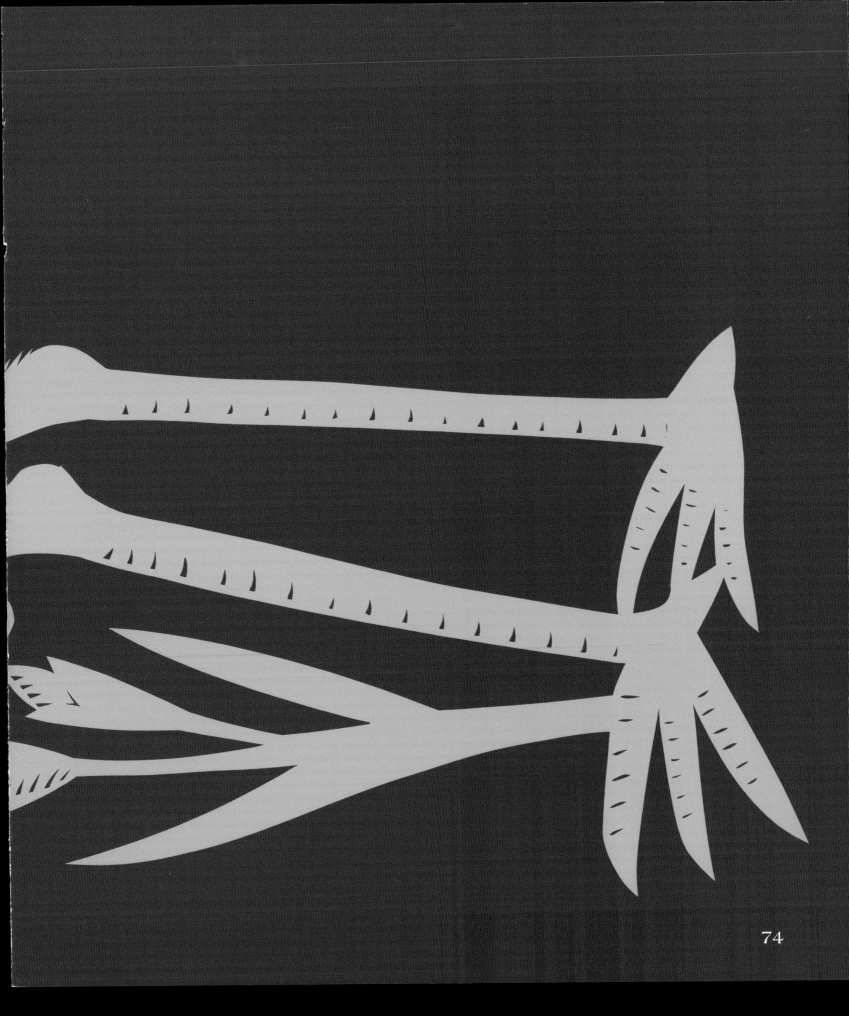

Persian Cypresses

Paper: smooth, black, colorfast, 20 lb. (or 80 gsm)

Dimensions, unfolded: 7 x 35½ in. (18 x 90 cm)

Tools: small precision scissors

Folding: in two

Cutting: follow the outline.

Persian Cypresses, displayed in shadow boxes. ⌃

Tree with Arabesques

Paper: smooth, black, colorfast, 20 lb. (or 80 gsm)

Dimensions, unfolded:
9 1/2 x 19 3/4 in. (24 x 50 cm)

Tools: art knife or scalpel

Folding: in two for the bottom six branches and on unfolded paper for the top.

Cutting: cut out the motif and finish with the outline.

Beetles

Paper: sienna-earth color, eggplant and purple, 32 lb. (or 120 gsm)

Dimensions, unfolded: 8 x 8 in. (20 x 20 cm)

Tools: small precision scissors, art knife or scalpel and 1/16- and 1/8-in. (2 and 3 mm) hole punches

Folding: in two

Cutting: cut out the pattern and finish with the outline.

Cut out several copies or several thicknesses of the pattern.

Beetles in 8 3/4 x 8 3/4 in. (22 x 22 cm) boxes painted with bright orange and gray acrylic paint, displayed on the facing page.

Overhead Panel

Paper: untearable, white

Dimensions, unfolded: 27½ x 78¾ in. (70 x 200 cm)

Tools: small precision scissors and art knife or scalpel

Folding: in four panels, each one 19¾ x 27½ in. (50 x 70 cm)

Cutting: cut out the motif and finish with the outline.

Keep the maximum number of connectors between the leaves, stems and insects to hold the cutout together.

Leave the outlining border intact to firmly hold the panel.

The panel set against a separate background of grayish-purple paper and hung from a curtain rod, displayed on facing page.

Thistles-in-a-Heart

Paper: smooth, red, 20 lb. (or 80 gsm)

Dimensions, unfolded: 19³/₄ x 19³/₄ in. (50 x 50 cm)

Tools: small precision scissors, art knife or scalpel, pinking shears and ³/₈-in. (1 cm) hole punch

Folding: in two

Cutting: cut out the motif and finish with the outline.

Cut out several copies or thicknesses of the pattern.

Tree
of Life

Paper: untearable,
white

**Dimensions,
unfolded:** 33 x 43 1/4 in.
(84 x 110 cm)

Tools: small precision
scissors and art knife or
scalpel

Folding: in two panels,
each one 16 1/2 x 43 1/4 in.
(42 x 110 cm)

Cutting: cut out the
motif and finish with
the outline.

Ganesha

Paper: smooth, white, 20 lb. (or 80 gsm)

Dimensions, unfolded: 10 x 12 1/2 in. (25 x 32 cm)

Tools: small precision scissors, art knife or scalpel, pinking sheers and 1/16-in. (2 mm) hole punch

Folding: in two

Cutting: cut out the pattern and finish with the outline.

Keep the connectors between the tree trunk, branches and animals to hold the cutout together.

Four Cranes in Flight

Paper: smooth, white, 20 lb. (or 80 gsm)

Dimensions, unfolded: 9 1/2-in. (24 cm) diameter

Tools: small precision scissors, art knife or scalpel and 1/16- and 1/8-in. (2 and 3 mm) hole punches

Folding: in four

Cutting: cut out the motif and finish with the outline.

Keep the connectors between the cranes and the outline to hold the cutout together.

Nasturtiums

Paper: smooth, white or colored, colorfast, 20 lb. (or 80 gsm)

Dimensions, laid flat: $8^7/_8$-in. (22.5 cm) diameter

Tools: small precision scissors and art knife or scalpel

Cutting: without folding the paper, cut out the motif and finish with the outline.

Round of Two Carps

Paper: smooth, white, 20 lb. (or 80 gsm)

Dimensions, unfolded: 9 1/2-in. (24 cm) diameter

Tools: small precision scissors, art knife or scalpel and 1/16- and 1/8-in. (2 and 3 mm) hole punches

Folding: in two

Cutting: cut out the motif and finish with the outline.

Keep the connectors between the carp and the border.

Round of Four Fish

Paper: smooth, white, 20 lb. (or 80 gsm)

Dimensions, unfolded: 9 1/2-in. (24 cm) diameter

Tools: small precision scissors, art knife or scalpel and 1/16- and 1/8-in. (2 and 3 mm) hole punches

Folding: in four

Cutting: cut out the motif and finish with the outline.

Keep the connectors between the fish and the border.

Japanese Flowering Quince with Butterflies

Paper: smooth, white, 20 lb. (or 80 gsm)

Dimensions, unfolded: 9 1/2 x 17 1/4 in. (24 x 44 cm)

Tools: small precision scissors, art knife or scalpel and 1/16-in. (2 mm) hole punch

Folding: in two

Cutting: cut out the motif and finish with the outline.

Cut out several copies or thicknesses of the pattern.

Keep the connectors between the butterflies, stems and flowers to hold the cutout together.

Bibliography

Allegri, Claude. *Louis Saugy*. Geneva: Les Editions du Ruisseau, 1977.

Lee, U-Fan. *Nostalgies Coréennes*. Paris: Réunion des Musées Nationaux and Musée Guimet, 2001.

Rta, Kapur Chisti and Rahul Jain. *Tissus Indiens*. Chicago: Paragon, 2000.

Zhilin, Jin. *L'Esthétique de l'Art Populaire Chinois*. Hong Kong: You-Feng and the Kwok on Museum, 1999.